ALWAYS EXTOLLING – A COLLECTION

Other Books by Don Davison
An Outline of a Philosophy of the Consciousness of Truth
The Concept of Personhood in the Evolutionary Process of Being
The Game of Life: A Player's Manual for Executives and Others
Sign Posts: A Collection of Essays, Vol. I
Sign Posts: A Collection of Essays, Vol. II
Sign Posts: A Collection of Essays, Vol. III

Poetry
Thoughts and Feelings Book I
Thoughts and Feelings Book II
Needles from the Ponderosas at Zirahuen
Seeds from the Ponderosas at Zirahuen
Pitch from the Ponderosas at Zirahuen
Humus from the Ponderosas at Zirahuen
Sawdust from the Ponderosas at Zirahuen
Sun's rays through the Ponderosas at Zirahuen
Shadows beneath the Ponderosas at Zirahuen
Cones from the Ponderosas at Zirahuen
Pollen sifting from the Ponderosas at Zirahuen
Reflections from Lucerne
Searching Swamps
Questions
Time's Echoes
Memories

Collections
Murmurings
Iris and Other Things
Pieces of the Journey
Through the Swamps of Time

ALWAYS EXTOLLING – A COLLECTION

Don Davison

Zirahuen
Phoenix, AZ
pathtotheself.com
DrDavison@pathtotheself.com

© 2005, 2010 by Zirahuen
All rights reserved. Published 2010
Printed in the United States of America.

ISBN 978-0-9774039-1-2

No part of this book may be used or reproduced in any manner whatsoever without written permission except in the case of brief quotations embodied in critical articles and reviews.

Cover photo by Keith Davison
Author photo by Patricia Davison

Special thanks to Louella Holter, Ron Redsteer, and Dan Boone at the Bilby Research Center of Northern Arizona University for editing and illustration services, and to Tina Rosio, from W.

For
Cristina,
David,
John,
and Keith

Perfect in every hue.
I believe in me
and I believe in you.

All of Don Davison's books have water on their covers. Water is one of the most essential attributes of the planet Earth; without it, life as we know it would not exist. It deserves our most considered attention.

Davison's collections of poetry all end with "Finding Pieces." Many of you have asked, where did the rules for the Game of Life come from? They come from many places and different times. Good hunting!

CONTENTS

The Hominid	1
Teeming Masses	2
Burnt Offering	4
Scriptoriums	6
On Gazing at a Maple Tree in Spring	7
Polis Mundi	10
In-Between Time	11
Touch	12
Reap the Wind	14
Cannon	15
And the Soul?	16
Seeing	19
Heroes	20
Stylus	22
Lamentations	23
What Good Am I?	24
The Pilgrim	27
Evening News	32
Thanatos	33
Culture's Cloak	34
Hezbollah – Jihad – Hamas	35
Transmigration	36
Love the Children	38
Epitaph	39
Men	40
Naked Faces	42

The Battle	43
Too Big	44
Postmodern Poets	45
Universities of the Next Millennium	46
Kosovo Manifesto	48
Fields of Sacrifice	49
Supplications of the Prophet	50
Humanity	52
Perpetrators	53
A Chance	54
To Cure the Wicked	55
Worth	56
The Paradox of Seeing and Believing	58
Wall Street Paragon	59
Life	60
A Request	61
Feeling Me	64
Intrusions	65
The All	66
The Truth	67
To Silence the Guns	68
Fear	70
War	73
Consumed	74
Academia	76
Sandunga	77
The Hearth	78
From the Mouth of the Cave	80
Vincent	81
The Formula	82
Oh – Dante Alighieri	83

I	84
Tears	85
Monk's Mutterings	86
The Hominid's Path	87
Who Is My Brother and My Sister?	88
Yes?	90
Conspiracy	91
Cold Light	92
The Mall	93
The Last Man	94
Freedom	95
Memories	96
Sea Shell	97
Pixel Stasis	98
60s 70s 80s 90s …	100
Voices of Humankind	101
Mother Nature	102
The Right	103
Life's Journey	104
Disturbing the Peace	106
To Those Who Lost …	107
Refugees	108
Soul's Search	109
I Want …	110
A Human Face – A Human Touch	111
Adoration	117
Mourning Song	118
Strike Force	120
The Wounds of Humanity	122
Sword and Shield	123

"Hawker of wares, what sell you but words?"
"Melodies of soul," I say.

THE HOMINID

                Fragments of bone
                Mounds of stone
                Scattered embers
                Heaps of sand
                Shards of clay
                Lumps of iron
                Slivers of glass
                Corroded copper
                Bits of tungsten
                Pieces of platinum

Jars of clay	Art works
Chariots of iron	Political systems
Pillars of stone	Philosophies
Stained glass	Architecture
Chalices of gold	Theologies
Cities of citizens	Symphonies
Towers of steel	Science
Satellites of alloys	Vanities

                Pieces of platinum
                Bits of tungsten
                Corroded copper
                Slivers of glass
                Lumps of iron
                Shards of clay
                Heaps of sand
                Scattered embers
                Mounds of stone
                Fragments of bone

TEEMING MASSES

There is such prodigious activity on the anthill of humanity.
How much of the anthill is visible to each one?
How much must we understand?
The pain of the intensity of the movement
takes so much from each soul.
To the individual, space and time is lost forever.
Who will teach the children of tomorrow
how to lie laughingly in the sun of summer?
Do we know where to begin?
We must stop rushing and turn into ourselves
before we rape them all!
How can we instill that needed measure of sensitivity
that breathes gently the sigh of *Truth*?
And what is it that so much activity produces?
Is it a finer linen tightly woven?
Do we know our present purpose,
or do we just push them all uncaringly toward the future?
Can we touch the gentle face of God
and be one with Him
and still rush them from cradle to grave,
brushing by the violet of Eternal Mystery?
I truly believe not,
for those so caught in the vortex,
but we must remember when the water boils
the mist gently rises to give birth
in its softness to another season.
We must turn the heat down!
Hope is so difficult to practice
when we see only the confusion of the present.
But we must!

We cannot forget that on the edge
and at the point of interface,
there is always a new beginning.
Paradox prevails – out of the old comes the new.
Breathe in serenity – teach them to stroll.
The anthill is all so visible
and we are responsible for the whole.
We must know that the music is created NOW!

BURNT OFFERING

Armies
Barrages
Sweat pours from brows
Fingers blister, pulling triggers
Insanity in history
Reality of war
A child
Trundling across the battle field
Volleys from both sides
A halo of bullets
A child
Struggling, running and stumbling
The middle of the battle
A cease fire
A child
Staggers and falls
Blood stains a ruddy face
Death takes a life much too soon
Regimental colors strike the ground
Screams cease
Smoke drifts
Burnt offerings to some lustful, awful god
Soldiers face their foe
Silence reigns
Throats ache
Eyes water
Guts rend
Death of many
Loss of a child
Zeal, yet sympathy

Rage of compassion
Men's feelings sweep the field
Madness and forgiveness
Despair from hope
Whirlwind of sentiment
Depths in truth
An afternoon
Valor to scorn
Beasts with hearts
Souls wanting homes

SCRIPTORIUMS

There were those remote cloisters,
hidden in valleys now deserted,
orders lost and vows forgotten.
They left buried in the sand
ancient rooms where on plain tables and hard benches,
a form with bent shoulders gave birth to scrolls in
a pregnant, focused silence amid flickering oil lamps.
Dedication to task with
stylus and parchment,
ink,
profound ideas,
elegant lines,
radiant forms,
sacred words.
Time laboriously spent.
A fortuitous protection.
Centuries expire.
The loupe and fragments,
truths etched from minds
emerge from the scatterings in the sand.

ON GAZING AT A MAPLE TREE IN SPRING

The smoothness of the bark,
the gentle softness of the leaves –
these are things that all call out to us.
Why have we forgotten to touch the world,
each other, and ourselves?
Is it because as we exploded around the globe
we have forgotten
how to speak in touching ways?
Wandering nomads, we left each other as we set about
searching for ourselves.
Crisscrossing continents and finding new shores,
we circumnavigated the globe in search of the Truth.
And then we populated every nook and cranny
using every conceivable ounce of human genius.
We colonized it all!
There were those who were there first,
but it never seemed to matter.
We pillaged and destroyed what we found
and reconstructed what we knew.
Cultures and pyramids,
crushed and recycled.
Many of our brothers and sisters
were sent to slave ships and to bondage.
Values subjugated to new icons of a different faith.
All to ferment and foment,
finally to give birth to *my* race, *my* religion, *my* country!
So the ugly head of nationalism gone berserk
screams and smells of smoke and death.
Touch has been such an essential aspect of evolution –
and we know that the process has been at itself for some time.

We must stay in touch with the movement of the species;
if anyone hurts, the pain is ours.
We must learn to be honest with the bullets.
If we shoot them we must own the consequence.
A sniper's or bomber's soul is blackened
when children and the elderly fall
on their way to go shopping or to school.
What purpose is there to the ignorance of the touch of
shrapnel or jacketed lead death?
To each there is that human moment when, if human,
we know right from wrong and we cry.
The eyes of the slaughterers (surely they are not soldiers)
are also wet
when evenings of honest sharing meet
God's dusking contemplation.
We must scream *YOU LIE!*
You who pull the triggers,
you who blaspheme in the face of the Truth.
Any person is your neighbor!
Bow to the Truth, you murdering bastards of humanity!
Remember to each murdering moment there is a corpus –
yours and the victim's.
To debate in ecumenical circles and procrastinate
when people die
is subhuman.
And so we have those bastards who do the killings,
and those who watch and talk about it.
We scream No!
And yet we hear the guns
in Northern Ireland,
the Middle East,

the Subcontinent,
Sub-Saharan Africa,
and Central America.
And the list goes on ...
to include each and every hamlet and megapolis.
We have lost the sense of touching self and others.
I reach out with tear-laden eyes to touch the maple tree
as the ocean's waves give birth to misty Springs
and the beauty of bark and leaves.

POLIS MUNDI

They stumble in long lines,
on trails, on roads, in camps,
carrying everything they own in small bundles.
They come from distant bush villages,
from mountain slopes,
from marshes and from gentle valleys,
from co-opted urban centers,
our brothers and our sisters,
the people of the world.
Refugees flow in perennial streams,
walking, staggering, carrying their children.
In never-ending, multicolored lines
the ethnic groups commingle.
We hear the muffled cries for help.
We hear the screams of death.
We see the dry dust on tear-stained faces.
We feel the incessant pain as bonds
of family and place are torn mercilessly asunder.
We are witnesses to the death of hope.
Stop the plunder of the species!
Stop the abhorrent tide of terror!
Save the cradles!
Save the flutes!
Save the music!
Save the children!

IN-BETWEEN TIME

We remember where we've been,
we know where we want to go.
Where are we? That's the question.
Have we been pushed into the now
because of where we've been?
Some because they love the moments of the past.
Some because they hate the memory of the past.
Some longing for some remembered shore,
a similar thing close to the past and always more than the past.
Some fleeing painful places, dark hurtful places,
pushing them towards never again!
and on to places filled with pleasure and peace.
The in-between time,
when suddenly we realize we are free,
moving with ourselves
towards another moment with ourselves.
Yes!
It's all a yes,
being, begetting being by being.
So now on that bridge of in-between time we realize,
it's all in-between time.
We are always, forever, on the bridge of life,
from where we've been to where we're going.
It's a gentle bridge, arching slightly,
rising over calm rivulets, ponds, raging rivers and stormy seas.
And yet we stand on the bridge and say,
"Yes! Cogito! Dasein! L'chaim! Vita!
Dreams! That's all …"

TOUCH

Touch is acknowledgment of being.
If your response is nothing,
how do I know you are with me?
I know you are there someplace.
I like knowing you are there.
We have talked, we have walked,
we have shared moonlight, water, music,
popcorn and ourselves.
Yes, we must talk, but touch mostly each other
on our walks or sitting gently by the fire.
Hold me!
Pull me towards you!
Cling for those mutual moments of ecstasy!
Linger long before and after!
There will be times when I will be gone.
There will be times when you will be gone.
We, however, can remember and our bodies can feel
those soft gentle acknowledgments of being.
We are two who found each other
in the wilderness of the universe's space and time.
We have touched each other in our now.
Touch is reciprocal,
I touch, you touch,
We touch,
You touch, I touch,
We touch.
I touch you and say,
"Yes! I am here with you now."
You touch me and say,
"Yes! I am here with you now."

I say yes to all that you are.
You say yes to all that I am.
We are two infinite and eternal beings,
two circles locked together.
Yet we know on the edges there are differences –
as there should be.
You are unique.
I am unique.
You must be faithful to your heart and your differences,
and so must I.
They are differences that are true but do not matter
when it comes to walking together.
The heart,
the soul,
the sharing of our being,
this is all that matters.

REAP THE WIND

Media moguls and prophets of profit, know this:
You reap the wind when you lie.
Always, dishonesty has given us crops of chaos
in which greedy gales of history's maelstroms
crush the innocent.
Our species' record of respect for those who are truly victims,
the forever young that come and come and come,
has too little charity.
When human needs are known, we must deliver the truth.
The crooked course of our past has always had two truths
– yours and mine –
and yet we know in the pit of our stomachs
there is truth that does not depend upon anyone.
It belongs to itself.
If only we, you and I, could stand still in silence
waiting upon the truth,
we could be beneficiaries of holy stuff.
When avarice is put to bed, we seldom fear for life.
All things are either
true or not true, mine or not mine.
Why then do we insist upon wallowing in ignorance?
Truth is a holy endeavor!
When we focus upon yesterday's gale,
we miss the calm of the present.
The silent dawn, the evening tide, all wait,
while caught in a paradigm of yesteryear,
we follow trails of dead leaves skittering in the wind.

CANNON

Heavy, laden with purpose,
smooth and sensuous to the touch,
the form sits on a grassy slope shrouded by fog,
its mouth agape to history.
Is its throat sore from belching,
roaring across field and glen, farm and glade?
I wonder if its memory is as hard as its iron heart.
What roaring heat from some hidden forge
gave birth to such things?
Whose artisan hands carved templates for the castings?
Does it remember those throngs of men
– brothers all –
who felt its terrible sting?
What scents and scenes cross its brow,
while the mist of time pits its polished skin?
What music did it hold for men
when cadence bound them to their souls in acts of war?
Fire! Fire! Fire!
And fire again!
Does the soul love rhythm so much
that it can't hear men's cries?
The grass glistens a silvery green.
Droplets coalesce on the blades.
A bundled child crawls up the brackets of stone
and sitting on the mighty cannon,
touches history.
With one hand on their shoulders
and the other stroking history,
will the children learn the truth
if we do not stand next to them,
eyes moist and tears streaking cheeks?

AND THE SOUL?

Where are the Mixtec, Tarahumara,
Aztec, Toltec, Chichimec and Lacandón warriors?
Where are the Mayan warriors and the others?
Who will defend the children, the mountains, the plains,
our bodies and our souls from the violators?
The moaning is becoming stronger,
the torture is almost complete.
We have lived with examples of thieves
from time immemorial.
Now the time has arrived,
listen well to the messages of the winds of antiquity:
The Patrón has become the thief.
He has taught us how to be thieves with everyone.
Where are the warriors of virtue?
Apparently, common and mundane virtue
is born of the sacred aspect of money.
It's obvious, isn't it?
No, my children, no!
From the parabola of statistics comes the Truth:
Everything lies between the X and the Y!
In each group there is someone who knows
and can say,
"No! No longer!"
Who is going to teach the children?
Who is going to stop and say, "No longer!"?
We have let them glorify evil, the low life of the spirit.
May the warriors of the spirit come!
Listen, everyone,
"Not any longer!"
We are all bastards and what difference does it make?

We have been for centuries,
from the time when we were in our tribes.
All of this was before there were priests,
before religions,
long before governments.
Listen!
There is no one who commands,
except the Truth.
And from the mountains of the Sierra de la Silla,
the mountains of Jalisco,
the mountains of Puebla and the mountains of Oaxaca,
comes reverberating the reparations
of Popocatepetl and Ixtacihuatl.
From the bubbling of the springs of all of the mountains
the message gushes forth,
carried in the voice of the past.
It comes crying, "Where are the warriors of the Truth?"
The peso is now worthless.
Who is responsible?
We are all responsible!
We have all been standing,
watching, while they bribe the Mexican people.
And although we no longer have any blood,
we still have sweat.
We are Mexicans to the bones!
They have stolen from us until there is no more meat,
but we have these bones!
From these bones we will make soup
and with this we will feed the soul,
the soul of the Truth.
May the warriors rise from their tombs!

Listen between the lightning bolts,
the voices of our ancestors,
they come screaming through the pine needles.
Where are the Mixtec, Tarahumara,
Aztec, Toltec, Chichimec and Lacandón warriors?
Where are the Mayan warriors and the others?
There is no Subcommander of anyone!
There is no Patrón of anyone!
There is no Government of anyone!
The only thing that remains is the human person,
with the soul shining,
brilliant with the Truth and responsible for itself.
From the north to the south,
out of the Sierra Madre
comes gently to the ear, the Truth! the Truth!
The time has died when we blame "the Others."
The hour has arrived for a populace that knows the Truth.
Finally, we have a vague, misty understanding.
Now we can hear in the cobwebs of the sepulchers,
from the heart of the pyramids,
now is the time to become owners of the Word:
The Truth! The Truth!

SEEING

The penumbra of the self
emerges from the cataclysmic,
attached to and part of the Brilliant Flash,
forcing participation in the effervescence of the universe's
dallying and triumphant sustaining push and pull.
Strings of the universe give us glimpses
of the unfolding efforts of God's Mind.
We aren't privileged to see them all –
we are connected to only a few.
Yet we know there must be others;
we, ourselves, are "another."
The penetration of our presence
in His Playground is forever small,
caught in visions, seeing only slices
in which the convoluted efforts
of the psyche and emotive are still warring.
We live encapsulated and saturated
by the physical (within and about).
The miracle is that we see something
with an equanimically magnanimous great synthesis,
all converging in the soul's light.

HEROES

Young daughters and sons ask, "Mommy, Daddy,
where do the heroines and heroes go when they get tired?"

* * *

The Regal Elk, impaled and weary,
beds exhausted next to the primeval pine.
Time healing wound's edges,
days come and days go.
The Great Wolf, slashed and bleeding,
curls deep in his den beneath the ancient spruce,
licking wounds, too sore to move.
Drifting in and out of sleep as starlight gives birth to dawns.
The Mighty Eagle, feathers missing, talons torn,
perches motionless on the rock shelf.
Winds blow, hail comes,
sunsets and moonrises
grace the stone's face.
The Warrior, arms cut and thigh gaping,
lies smearing mud upon his wounds, resting in a grotto,
weeks flow in silent prayerful passing.
Others, not knowing, wait in painful hope.
The Lady, motionless, beaten, raped and brutalized,
sits scorned for her commitment to faith and family.
With uncommon strength she nurtures herself in a strange land.
Mate and family,
disoriented without her presence,
pray for her return.

* * *

Where have heroines and heroes gone?
To sacred places, every one!
Each has had their lair or den,
cliff's edge or peak.

Needing moments of repose
from life's tumultuous undertakings,
weary and spent in deeds of need and valor,
all have sought to rest.
Children, hear us now, the time will come
when you too will tire and grow weary on life's long path.
Heed the voices of the winds.
Find your lair, den, cliff's edge, garden, peak or glen.

STYLUS

Slice the flesh!
Let the rivulet run!
With a sliver split from oaken bonds,
the fragile lines I write.
Single letters forming words, thoughts –
all feelings captured in the rust of serum and corpuscles.
Slice again!
Let the rivulet flow!
The power of the pen drives fingers –
pushing, pulling, dragging sentences across pages.
What racks the soul,
stirs the Mighty Sword of Truth?
In the dimming light
the cu-cu-ru-cu-cu of the mourning dove is all I hear.
Binding wounds I wait, ready,
the Sword will move again.

LAMENTATIONS

Who will build barns for the next generation?
Those stalwart shelters
protecting life and forage from the elements
now sit slanting in the winds of time.
Where will the soft noises of rumination be housed
when masonry and concrete walls with no roofs,
no doors, no windows
lie up against forgotten hillsides
with thistles gracing gaping holes
through which life's movements passed?
Abandoned manure mounds covered with the season's finery
hold treasure from the process.
A faint essence issues forth only in spring and fall
when moisture makes its presence
and roses need their supplement.
Now it's Mega Barns for Mega Foods,
all corrugated aluminum, steel, and concrete
with fiberglass, green and opaque, dotting roofs and sides.
An insipid finish, dull,
a washed pastel where weathered wood once stood.
Aluminum, stainless steel, graphite fibers,
Plexiglass and photovoltaic
will shelter sojourners as they move to the great beyond.
Where in Battle Star Galactica will barns be tucked away?
When will the winds of the seasons wick again
the moisture from our brows?

WHAT GOOD AM I?

The airport was small, a wayside between nations.
Awaiting a shuttle, I stopped for a cup of tea.
Choosing an empty table along the wall near the corner,
I looked forward to a moment of repose.
It was then that the sound came to me,
barely audible,
some murmurings, or a shuffling of feet, I thought.
Then, I saw him.
An old – ancient would be better – man
with weathered skin and white, tousled hair,
hunched over a table in the corner.
A cup sitting on the table was firmly held in both hands.
He was uttering,
"What good am I?
What good am I?
I can no longer smell scents of the seasons,
no longer taste the spice of meals.
I can't hear sounds of laughter.
Conversations of my friends have grown silent.
They are all dead,
and would it be that I could hear them if they weren't.
What good am I?
What good am I?
The numbness and trembling in my fingers
makes holding a cup of soup
impossible.
I spill most of it down my front.
To use a spoon is to waste the food.
What good am I?

What good am I?
To hold a woman,
I have none.
To stroke the head of a child,
there aren't any.
To climb the mountain, I am unable.
What good am I?
What good am I?"
The supplications were repeated over and over
as he sat holding the cup that seemed frozen to the table.
And I, glued to my chair with embarrassment,
participated in his monologue.
The thought occurred to me that I had whispered
the same question,
What good am I?
in moments of tension and distraught when
I had so much of everything he lacked.
The droning
of his litany continued
and I found myself asking
some unknown god,
What can I do?
What good am I
if I can't do something?
My rational mind chided me with the truth.
I couldn't give him back
lost senses,
his mate,
or family and friends.

There was nothing I could do,
except share with him
that his plight had reminded me
of my lameness, my smallness,
in the face of the absurd and difficult.
When having everything
I had feigned having nothing.
Engulfed in waves of guilt,
I determined to share the meaning his message had for me
and to thank him.
Approaching his table I saw his head resting on his arms,
eyes closed.
I coughed slightly to rouse him
and when there was no movement I touched him gently.
Cold skin told me his prayer had been answered.

* * *

Years later –
when approaching a new class of young minds,
too youthful to know,
too quick to judge,
easily led into despair,
I find myself saying, "I sat in an airport once …"

THE PILGRIM

Haggard and filthy, clothes torn,
eyes but blood-stained, hollow sockets,
he came stumbling and crawling down the well-worn path.
The madness of war
and moments of rivalry spent in debauchery
were all he knew.
Years thus spent had sapped his strength.
The three denizens of mortal life
– war, wine, and women –
had left only
a creature resembling a man.
Yet, when the sun set
and the stillness of the evening fell upon the earth,
a bent form paused at the side of the road,
the corner of the square, wherever,
and somewhere in those weary, faded blue eyes
a faint hint of a glint would stir fleetingly
and go unnoticed to any who hurried by.
And so it was,
late one evening when raging torrents
crashed upon the countryside,
this forgotten soul,
who had stopped to huddle beneath an ancient spruce
just off the beaten path, heard a gasping, grating call
drifting through the intermittent clashes of the thunder
and the swishing of the downpour,
"Help me! Please help me!"
Rousing himself from exhaustion,
he scrambled from his sanctuary
and rushed into the blackness of the night.
The sound came to him a bit stronger now as he hurried on.

Finally,
finding himself at the edge of a roaring river,
he assessed that the cries came from somewhere
in the raging waters.
Shielding his eyes against the wind and rain
he saw through a flash of lightning
a small child clinging to a rock,
just upriver from where he was leaning over the bank.
He shouted to the youth,
"I will stretch out from the bank and catch you
when you come by."
Sliding down the slippery rocks, he grabbed a hanging branch
and wading into the shallows,
stretched out his hand and yelled to the child, "Let go!"
As the child slipped into the boiling current,
he bent as far as he could into the cold, rushing river
and catching sight of a bobbing hand,
clutched it with every bit of strength
he had in his tired body.
Then, pulling the child to the riverbank, he heard him say,
"Amen."
Scooping the wet and cold form into his arms,
he scurried back to the shelter of the spruce.
Laying the small form on his tattered and torn cloak,
he rubbed the child's hands, arms and legs.
It wasn't until the shock of the exertion wore off
that he noticed the child was dead.
Covering the corpse,
he sat dazed as his mind roamed through his past
searching for some reason
to the things of life's deepest moments.

He remembered many years ago,
when he was young,
watching an old monk kneel all day long,
from the crispness of the dawn through the heat of the day,
into the still, dampness of the evening.
Yet all he ever heard him say was,
"And the child said, 'Amen.'"
He had reflected,
Why would he do this:
Kneel all day
on a ledge of stone
and repeat such a thing?
What good did it do
to say, Amen?
Now, as his mind returned to the present,
he picked up the bundled body
and sat holding it next to his heart.
He had no family, no sons, no daughters, no one.
He rocked back and forth slowly.
The rain turned to sleet, then to snow.
Numbness crept into the core of his broken body.
His mind began drifting far beyond his many yesterdays
to the Crusades and to the final battle at Jerusalem.
Amidst the foray and chaos of the fighting,
he struck down a Moor.
In a momentary reprieve from the din,
kneeling beside his dying enemy,
as his lifeblood gurgled forth, he heard him whisper,
"And the child said, 'Amen.'"
Then a long-forgotten day of his youth
sifted through his mental fog.

Passing through north Italy
on the way to the Holy Land
late one evening,
he had come upon a group of brigands
who had absconded with a harlot from a nearby town.
They had set upon her with the worst of manners
and having had their way with her, beaten her nearly to death.
Driving them off,
he was as fearless a warrior as any of the best;
he washed her wounds and covered her with his cloak.
In the early morning she roused slightly
and as she took her last breath,
she said in a clear, bell-like tone,
"And the child said, 'Amen.'"
He recalled the feeling of awe that struck him
as he thought of the brutality
and savagery of the brigands
in their disrespect for another's life.
For her to have uttered the same words of the old monk
as well as the dying Moor was strange.
That was not all –
In a skirmish with bandits a troop of soldiers were well tested
and several badly wounded,
including his close friend Guy Morrow.
He had cleansed his wound and laid him by the fire.
Having wrapped him in the robes of his fellows,
he set about to comfort him.
The young Guy had asked haltingly about the saints and hell.
Telling him there was no concern,
that he would live many years and have scores of offspring,
he busied himself about the fire.

At about the twelfth hour Guy sat bolt upright
and said in a strong voice, "and the child said, 'Amen.'"
Then, falling back in his saddle, he never took another breath.
What was this thing about a child
and what did this word "Amen" really mean?
Swirling thoughts in memory's mist
left these questions unanswered
as his body shed its warmth and strength.
All he could feel and hear now
were his mother's gentle hands and sweet, soft voice
as she cradled him and sang about a child,
and … and … and …
His consciousness faded
and his eyes focused only on the lacy cascade of snowflakes.
A young monk,
hurrying on an appointed task,
paused momentarily
at the sight of the wretched old man and the child.
Approaching slowly, he saw
fading blue eyes glaze over and he heard him murmur,
"And the child said, 'Amen.'"

EVENING NEWS

Is it the penchant of poets
to wallow in the triflings of their age?
Wars come,
serenity ceases, rage revels,
lives spill blood of another's life,
wars go.
So cheap the commodity of truth,
we expect it on the newsprint of the evening,
to be consumed while our pounding hearts race
in the wake of noise and movement?
Or,
must poets
turn their hearts
toward better things?
Truth
and tranquility
settle in the leaves and grasses of time.
Loons still call.
Cottontails nibble shoots.
Minnows dart in shallows.
Moonrises come in the east.
Why then choose to believe
all life's truths come in black smudges on newsprint,
speaking of things
that have not bothered you all day?

THANATOS

There is such joy in life,
could there be death?
All life carries the seed of death.
Is this so that we feel deeply the gifts of the present,
or is it that, in the present, we sense the joy of eternity?
Thanatos, thou speaketh,
not because I want to hear your voice,
but because you come.
There is a heaviness in my chest,
not because I want to stop,
but because I'm tired.
I have scurried through the halls of life
from room to room,
and now it seems it's time to go.
Thanatos, you speak again,
I hear you.
And the children?
In the brilliance of their limpid pools
do I see your shadow
at the edges?
Would it be that smiles would not fade from the face of death
and we could meet eternity as we lived life?
Ready!

CULTURE'S CLOAK

A tapestry of overpasses,
underpasses,
highways, footpaths
and bike trails
passing through glen, village, town, metropolis,
watched by vagrants, by the lost,
next to abandoned buildings, junked vehicles,
amidst desolation.
They say:
"Dried bread crumbs aren't only pigeon fare …"
"Aluminum cans are more than just convenient …"
Pails and barrels belching smoke and soot
warm hands and feet.
Crowded bus stations are where weary eyes question:
"Where do all the shiny cars go?"
"Penthouses, I guess."
"Worn shoes with thin soles
let you feel your path upon the earth."
"I've never learned how to wash without water.
You can't go to a laundry and stand naked."
"God bless the rain!"

HEZBOLLAH – JIHAD – HAMAS

Anger, now!
Critical mass, now!
Someone knows, now!
Can they be loving brothers and sisters?
To whom must we lie? To whom can we lie?
To hate the infidel in the now is to be blind
to the Heart of Allah,
the Compassionate, the Merciful.
Peace is to sense the serum of the Divine.
Allah is praised!
We are a piece of life flowing towards more life.
Fed by the Holy One,
Allah is praised! Peace is with you!
They all nurtured the many:
Socrates – The peace of the Parthenon,
Buddha – A shred of the Pipal tree,
Confucius – Mist congealing to Sacred Rivers,
Christ – The Cross,
Mohammed – A rock of the Cave of Enlightenment.
The birth sin is the desire to be
other than.
Life is suffering when
other than.
Extinguish the inmost desire to be
other than.
We are all glowing embers igniting
the Flame of Belief.

TRANSMIGRATION

They were here,
the natives and the others.
"Savages," some were called.
"Foreigners," "Mexicans."
Their ways were different.
Always,
a great boiling pot of space and opportunity
beckoned to those across the sea.
They swallowed stories of myth and legend and they came.
Some came seeking fortune,
some seeking adventure.
Some because there was no place in the field or shop,
some because there was no food.
Always memories of the Homeland died hard.
Heroic efforts were made to acquire a new tongue,
years spent losing accents.
"Become an American!"
When we become something else
do we know where we are going?
And why, if it's such a wonderful place,
do we always think of home?
Was it ever as real as our heart said it was,
or just an amalgam of dreams?
Whatever the reason, we came –
with languages and customs.
Ours were ours – theirs were different.
Always someone saying they – theirs –
was less than,
even wrong.
We were suspicious.
Were they out to steal my few possessions?
Were they here to kill me, or mine?

Take away my opportunity?
Or were they trying to ridicule my difference?
Yes, in some cases it was all true.
We rekindled a deep sense of watchfulness –
something touched a primitive anxiety
and resurrected primal emotions of fear and anger.
Yet this amalgam,
this burnished and polished vessel of new culture,
has produced men and women saints,
great artists and poets,
statesmen and entrepreneurs.
And still we look askance at differences.
Still we debate immigration.

LOVE THE CHILDREN

They come into being
everywhere,
all the time.
They come from pristine jungles,
on the edges of everything,
in urban conglomerates.
They come crying.
They come laughing.
They come from hurtful places,
from indifferent environs,
from caring hands.
They all come
with fears and hopes.
Crawling, walking, running away from pasts to futures,
they come smiling,
they come grimacing,
from pleasant journeys,
from unhealthy circumstances,
from the arms of love.
They all come apprehensively
seeking, peeking, striking out,
poised
for today and tomorrow.

EPITAPH

Better red than dead!
What have we read?
Plato, Kant, Marx, Pope Leo XIII, Kierkegaard,
People's Magazine and the *National Inquirer*.
We live wanting so desperately to be led.
What difference will it make when we are all dead?
The Rebellion of the Masses.
Into what?
Where is the mystery,
Holy,
Communalism,
Socialism,
Nationalism,
Materialism,
Paternalism,
Feminism,
and finally, Fraternalism?
Will we all wake up and realize we have had the wrong faith?
Did we know what to hope for?
Fundamental needs conflict with numbers and time.
The ideal must become some of the real:
The All = A Few / A Few = The All.
We have not learned what to give.
Hope is what we try to give a child, isn't it?
The agony of a people is in not finding a way to give,
and still we hear,
"How long does it take to rewind the movie?"

MEN

Being's mandate:
Kill or be killed.
Thus driven for millennia,
we still take harbor in this shadow.
Men are loins and hearts,
both with personal history.
Winds of the passionate and temperate
whirl through us as deeds.
We are the ritual keepers for our brothers,
passers on of sacred rites,
goblet masters
and torch bearers.
Too little now do we sit around the fire
tearing off fetters of silence,
beating our chests,
bathing cheeks in tears.
Our life journey must be shared,
the old with the young,
the young with the old.
How else would we know how to own the despair
and ecstasy of our sojourn?
Though we set out eons ago,
only small remnants of piled and worked stone,
some for housing, some for killing, some for cutting,
as well as those haunting images of Lascaux and Altamira
hint of our epic.
As new centuries begin, we start by looking back.
How far is far enough?
Scratching the thin film of the past
cannot touch the truth.
Too many stone structures shadow much of our naked soul.
Our line of survival is marked by leaving tracks upon the land
in places of Gomagh,*
and firm touches in the forests of men,
especially on their hearts.

Where do we start?
So deep is the message of connection
in the webbing of the genes.
The roar of the saber-toothed tiger
does not begin to share the truth of the trials.
It is so much more than that.
Our courage was shaken and yet our resolve was not destroyed.
There is nothing more tremendous than a man alone.
Quivering senses stir recollections,
and we remember the rushing in our organs
as we swam in the primordial soup
of the anthropoid and hominid.
And too, there is nothing so marvelous
as when two men work together.
The edge, although keen, is less sharp.
They both keep watch.
If the "Others" come, back to back we will defend
ourself and our brother.
From the depths of canyons, heights of craggy peaks,
banks of swollen rivers, sands of heated deserts,
knowing the omnipresent shadow of death
lingered at the edge of every eye,
we must scream, "Yes!" for all our brothers.
A profound connection of being
infuses us with a breath that bursts forth as a "One, Now!"
The current message and meaning of our presence,
as the word becomes flesh and as the world becomes one, is:
Love is a necessity, not a luxury.

* A Gomagh is an earth-shaking, adrenaline-rushing, soul-stirring event.

NAKED FACES

Youth's luster left as scattered pieces.
Scaling incessant petty peaks and participating
in the omnipresent onslaught of noise,
all is lost.
They stand staring, streaked with tension,
dripping anger down weathered, time-worn cheeks
blackened with loneliness
and glowering.
Where is the robust countenance?
I see droves of pallid, flat, insipid faces,
rushing streams, a gamut of pale semblances,
too many naked faces dressed only with dead eyes.

THE BATTLE

They call it simply a clash of cultures.
Don't they know how deep the pain?
When Whistling Hawk wandered the breaks of the plains,
eyes encompassing the gifts of the Great Spirit,
face touched by the wind,
ears tuned to the secrets of the silence,
was he not one of God's creatures
who splashed across the meandering courses of His streams?
They were not called Braves because they had no heart.
They were not called Soldiers because there was no purpose.
Oh, Great Spirit!
It is so difficult to know the depths of each sacred chapter,
so difficult to remember …

Whistling Hawk	Corporal Edwards
Red Hand	Lieutenant Black
Running Dog	Sergeant Muldoon
Falling Feathers	Captain McPee
Two Bears	Private Smith

… and all the others.

TOO BIG

From the fatigue of my time and place,
fettered to an unknown purpose,
a shadow bathes me in a heavy weariness.
My heart aches.
There are too many, there is so much.
I wish I had been born with a smaller heart.
Caught in the euphoria of mystery,
I am bowed by a great tiredness
as I wander the highways and byways.
And then ...
Suddenly, caught in the corner of my eye,
I see a scrambling porcupine,
or the bashful smile of a child.
Oh God!
Which corner could I leave out?
What chamber should I not fill?

POSTMODERN POETS

Cacophonous ruminations of mind and matter,
some from disconnected pens of apathy
and not a few postmodern poets,
break silent dawns and evening times when spirits soar.
Awash in the group think of their time,
may a stillness recapture their senses, may they bathe in
the profound silence of eternal music,
always set beyond the day's temporal convergence,
always open,
always free.
The Temple will not be built
of the noise of shattered stones.
It will forever be of one peace.

* * *

And you may ask pontificatingly
from the sea of rational machinations,
the "Big Bang?"
To which I say,
"backdrop melody for lark, sparrow and wren."

UNIVERSITIES OF THE NEXT MILLENNIUM

What role for the universities of the next millennium,
just laboratories,
research centers,
cobwebbed hubs for Web-Streamed Everything?
Will cyberpunks and cyborgs
(the next several generations of each)
have saturated the surf with individualized opportunities
for further fractualization of the hominid's
penchant for groupiness?
Will familial anything be necessary?
Is intercourse (of any kind) to become only "entertainment"?
Will simulacrum have its way?
Yes! No! I do not know!
Will the post - postmodern era
be one of increasing groups of young minds
having feasted too long at the teledildonics table,
that they are so obese with hedonism
they will not be fit for potato salad?
Will the thin film of the past
be shaved into still-thinner slices of the now,
becoming a single frame of compressed reference?
Not so much because no one can check into history,
but because we are creating so much data.
Who will have time to "turn their back"
on the cresting waves of Data Smog*
and spend time reflecting on what is *really real*?
Whereto for those individuals choosing
to wear their own personhoods?

* *Data Smog*, David Shenk

And what is it called
when something goes so fast it leaves itself behind
and becomes nothing staring at nothing?
Will there be only background noise
and the eclectic movement of electrons' darting shadows?
Or …
is this to be the golden age where higher education precipitates
quality and fraternalism,
a paradise of pilled pleasures without inspiration
– the genome having bequeathed all her secrets –
who will know the meaning of dis-ease?

KOSOVO MANIFESTO

As those
who with wanton maliciousness were driven from their homes,
may a firmly resolved effort of resettlement and immigration
forge a new bond of human unity.
One that relentlessly excises
the Arkans of Malevolence.
May the nurturing of a truly human presence,
with respect for the diversities of humanity
and a common commitment to the land and body politic,
focused on the soft impact of the human presence,
become the legacy
of an insidious policy of ethnic cleansing.
And
may this exercise
in humanity's individual and corporate struggle,
become a beacon of vigilance.
If a nation must be brought to its knees
because of an enforced ignorance
or apathetic disregard for others,
then –
so be it.

* * *

In the ecumenical spirit of nature's abundance,
let it be known:
No one suffers and dies in vain.

FIELDS OF SACRIFICE

On the battlefields of all our wars
they lay on the bosom of her breasts,
the dead and dying.
You drew their flowing blood deep into your damp womb,
in order to give birth to yet another generation
who will "hold opinions"
for which they, too,
will be willing to do battle and to die.
There stands a mighty oak bearing witness to it all.
In passing, awestruck by its majestic form,
every creed and race bowed before
its great, purposeful presence.
Slowly, deep from the depths of the hominid's soul,
realizations bore fruit.
We are all too much the same to have so many differences.
An age came to pass.
We've all been touched by their sacrifice.
Begs the question …
Will the touch finally be enough to bring
each and every one of us
to an eternal vigilance that maintains an ever-present
respect for life?

SUPPLICATIONS OF THE PROPHET

Eyes flowing great tears,
the Prophet wept.
Standing tall, hands extended to the heavens,
and finally falling to his knees,
voice raised,
he said,
"In the name of Allah,
the Compassionate, the Merciful,
You are praised! Oh Holy One! You are praised!"
Bowing his head to the ground, he prayed:
"I beseech you, Oh Holy One,
You are praised.
These are not mine!
Whosoever cannot worship the beauty of Your Creations,
be praised,
is not a follower of the Precepts.
War was only a tool when we could not communicate.
In today's world
it must be used only to save the lives of the innocent.
Holy Warriors –
terrorism is not a part of
the Path to Your Way.
Allah, be praised!
The Compassionate, The Merciful."

* * *

The clouds of unknowing parted and a voice said,
"Provide for the less fortunate.
Benevolence with magnanimity is the only way.
Allah be praised,
the Compassionate, the Merciful, be praised."

* * *

And the Prophet wept for
the indiscriminate deaths of the many children,
wept for the women,
wept for the old men, and wept for his fellow warriors.
The wind swept his words across the seas
and they did not hear them.
There were those too weak to care,
those too ignorant to love,
who could not feel the pain
of the Prophet's heaving lungs.
Centuries have passed,
yet if one who is devout listens carefully,
they can still hear the Prophet weeping.

HUMANITY

If anyone wants to sense a piece of the human effort,
come and stand next to a trestle and see, feel and hear
the iron horse galloping along rails
that stretch across continents.
Or,
stand among the stone and concrete canyons of the great cities
and sense the bustle and hustle behind the walls.
Or better yet ...
stroll upon the walkways of the world at quitting time
and be jostled by your brothers and your sisters
and laugh and cry.

PERPETRATORS

Men, women, young, old, every race, every creed –
all are victims.
Where is the hue and cry from the Imams, Mullahs,
Patriarchs, Popes, Clerics, Preachers and Priests,
Monks and Nuns?
Biophilia! Biophilia!
It is the very sacredness of life that we all profess –
and so ignore.
We come late to the table of magnanimous compassion.
Too long have we felt ourselves sequestered
by culture's ugly lassitude,
that bigotry of ignorance, that conscious self-avoidance
leading us all to lonely deaths
and no understanding of the beatific.
In our shallow thinking, in our eclectic, fleeting deeds,
in our insipid wonderings,
we lack that simple depth of purpose,
honoring the efforts of the All.
Accumulating secular applications
of knowledge's shadowed purpose,
we have slaughtered and ignored the slaughtering
of every single thing.
Their screams, heard only by a saintly few,
meant nothing to most of the rest
of our brothers and our sisters of the world.
Moaning in prayerful hubris, we hunched our backs
and turned away from any form of hope and love.
To you bastards of no purpose, I scream into your ears,
"Stop the pilfering of the Divine treasure chest!
Save the children!"

A CHANCE

The 21st century persons' swashbuckling gaits
move them from economic summits,
taking place in the wake of terrorist activity and war,
to great financial fraud and environmental crises.
Yet in all this there is the chance
– mind you now –
a chance,
that from deep within a lost and fettered soul
waits a holy moment.
Suddenly, from a clearing cloudy sky,
there falls gently a butterfly.
And as it passes, sends a soul into rapture
by the buffeting of its tattered wings.
Torn from the earth and spun towards the heavens
a soul sees an unobstructed, ideal scene,
with the sun at its center.
What serendipitous moment!
Seasons of moments!
Could present themselves in a series of forevers,
giving one an opportunity to dream?

TO CURE THE WICKED

Would it be …
That humane potential is ripened in the vineyard of time
and that the righteous could withhold punishment,
even unto death,
and in so doing be forced to remind themselves that they
– the evil ones –
are still here, and there.
And to restrain them is a commanded obligation.
Perhaps to chain them to a tree with blanket and food,
so they must bear witness to the fullness
of the passing of the seasons.
And periodically,
we would be bound to approach them and ask,
"Are you ready?"

WORTH

An hour, a day, a week,
bits and pieces
of our time,
all spent to maintain life.
Rupee, mark, dollar, sol or yen,
what value to a person,
when life's blood is spent in labor,
yielding too little to survive?
What predicates a person's worth?
Are not life's needs the same for each and every one?
I greet each dawn with some desire to behold the evening time.
Is this a remnant attached from me to God's Great Cloak?
If this is so, then why am I not worth that of my next of kin?
Is the color of my skin a bondage,
or my size or sex the prison to which I am condemned?
Do I eat less and like "the good things" any less
than my brethren?
Why is this grand mystery a part of every place and time?
Have I not struggled long enough,
worked hard enough,
to deserve a full measure?
The gods speak of that "Eternal Time,"
When to each will come their all.
Is this to be my life's dessert,
a sometime, there and then?
I sweat and feel muscles sore and torn,
weary of the days.
Sun's rays and rain's dampness have all had their chance.
To what am I doomed?
What must I become?

Is there some magic formula,
an incantation that bestows "the good things" on us all?
I wait and see the hours move and my value stays the same.
I think that some enchanted demon sits upon my soul.
And yet from some deep recess,
a pocket lined with silver and with gold,
there comes a message saying;
"You belong to me and this is all that matters."
Sustained by this chasm's gift I feel a value all my own.
The sun's rays warm my body and speak to ears within.
The raindrops cleanse the dust
from limbs that light the incense
for my God.
"I live now, not I, but He lives within me."

THE PARADOX OF SEEING AND BELIEVING

If we need light to see –
why are we blinded by the light?
So we may choose to believe.
And what would that be, Master?
How many of you are there?
One!
Where are you?
Here!
When are you here?
Now!
Who is responsible?
For that, Master, there is only me, here, now!
Yes!
There is only for each and every one a yes,
breathed gently, forcefully spoken, shouted,
or screamed into God's face.

WALL STREET PARAGON

Media moguls insist on the play of the day.
Inexperienced young reporters run rampant
in the muck of the moment.
What will the legacy of the barons of business be,
a billion here, a headline there?
Who cares?
And yet ...
In the dust of history they will ask,
"Whose tracks are these?
Where do they go?"
Some go to prison, some to philanthropy with a purpose.
Integrity of mission and of intent,
the real bottom line,
a good, needed product,
an excellent, honest service,
these are the things that really matter.
These are the building blocks of the new foundations
for us all.
Only great men and women leave these tracks
in the hearts,
minds,
and souls of others.
All other tracks are incidental scuff marks scraped
across God's eyes.

LIFE

"Yes!"

A REQUEST

If I were to say to you,
"Light a candle so that you can see a way to the truth,"
would you understand what I mean for you to do,
expect you to do, and want you to do?
Some would have a measure of understanding
about the purpose and project;
some would not.
Let's see if we can clarify this for most of us.
I think it's fair to say there have been some individuals
across the millennial horizons
who have better understood this human thing,
this pilgrimage of births,
this journey through life's seasons,
death and beyond.
It is prudent that we become aware of some of their signposts
and walk in some of their footsteps.
Yes, we know they lived in different times
and in many different places.
It matters not,
the subject of human life
is a generic moment that encompasses us all.
And while we many times feel we are exceptional,
I believe the truth is,
we are unique representatives of the human family.
This being the case,
there should be much that would interest us
about our brothers and our sisters.

Their myths and legendary treks,
remnants of their archeological statements
as well as their many current contributions,
can serve to inspire us to make some
complementary personal statement with our presence.
Prejudice is a chasm away from prudence
and so it must be with an equanimical,
ecumenical if you will,
heart that we look to the shores of history
and choose our traveling companions.
We must also be aware that false pride,
which in any case is a deadly involvement
that robs us of all chance to learn to wear our personhoods,
must always be our denizen.
It is with this in mind
– the desire to wear well these hoods –
that we need to be about looking to our fellow travelers,
those who have made this trip before us.
Shepherd or merchant, royal or peasant, man or woman,
child or adult, race or religion,
it matters not.
The way of our life lies out before us as a golden path,
an opportunity to discover the beauty of ourselves,
our brothers, our sisters and the world.
Observations are many, mandates few.
Know thyself and to thine own self be true.
Love your neighbor as yourself.
Know your place in the universe,
or, at the very least, in this current earthly home.
Take off some of the old, put on some of the new.

There is Truth,
a Way,
and there is Light.
Seek the Truth,
and the Truth will set you free.
In an age of skepticism and cynicism
we have difficulty in comprehending the full meaning
of these joyful statements.
It is with this in mind that we must all learn to say graciously
to each and every one:
"L'haim!
To you and yours, to mine and theirs, to each and everything,
a yes to all life, now and forever!"

FEELING ME

I love stones.
I am a bridge.
Sometimes I feel that I span a river in England,
or from the mainland to an island in the sea.
A rock brought over as Viking ballast,
exchanged at the cost of blood and life
and finally to be set in a privileged place.
A piece of the arch that allows one to move
from here to there.
As part of the arch, I sink into myself
in order to support the weight that provides
the footpath from the known to the unknown.
In my place of pressure,
sensing my surroundings as I do,
I feel roots that reach into a deep and
distant past and hands that extend out into space,
seeking the continuance of the effervescence
of the process of being, becoming.
I am a bridge.
I love stones.

INTRUSIONS

World watchers are like dancing musicians on a bubble,
marveling at the colors swirling beneath their feet.
Ignorant of the tremendous internal pressure,
awaiting the penetrating prick of information.

THE ALL

In the far, cold reaches of space, a spark spits forth
and ignites the next breath of the universe.
An explosion equaling googolplex hydrogen bombs
creates a holocaust that flashes across time,
and slowly begins to congeal in the sensuous undulations
of solar winds that will eventually wind and twist
the interstellar dust into stars and galaxies,
populated by planets that will become homes
for creatures as soft as snails.

THE TRUTH

Pick your edge of the organic whole
and reach for fuller being,
which must result in closer union for the whole.
They have said it's so.
Please make it so!
Whether we are imploding or exploding doesn't matter,
the movement is the same.
The challenge is to maintain the integrity of the process,
all of it.
As Socrates said, shortly before he drank the hemlock,
"I recall an ancient prayer –
As it was in the beginning, is now, and ever shall be."
Is the only frame of reference going to always be
the memory of those fleeting moments
when we touched the leading edge,
and then were spun off into the mass to sustain
ourselves in base activities
until that next gratuitous movement
that places us again at the leading edge,
or is there a Golden Thread that penetrates us all
and whose light shines on
the Path forever?
Are these just lingering thoughts of
Feelings and Truth?
Perhaps, but where are those answers
that are seemingly the Keys
that are needed to sustain my focus?
Abba,
"Is my cry the answer?"

TO SILENCE THE GUNS

The falling of the water,
the rustle of the wind,
the cry of the hawk.
What was it that the Whiteman wanted?
What were they looking for?
They never seemed to stay in any one spot
long enough to enjoy it,
much less get to know it.
They were strange creatures
who did not seem to speak to any God.
It took time to let the Gods get to know you.
To do this you had to be still and listen,
to sit and watch.
You must stay in one place long enough to meet them.
Everyone knows that the Gods do not
present themselves all at once.
There is time in the Gods' tales and one must wait to hear it all.
The great bear rolls in the grass and laughs at the bees.
One does not know this
when one does not take the time to wait, to see and to listen.
So the warriors nocked their arrows,
painted their faces,
sang their chants and readied their ponies.
What had the Old One said?
Many things,
but what he said at the end was that we must silence the guns.
They roared in the faces of the Gods.
They broke the silent contemplation of the maidens.
They disturbed the stillness of the young men's trials.

They echoed like the thunder across the valleys,
and there was always something dead
when the noise was heard no more.
After the thunder, the rain came
and washed the faces of the Gods.
This Whiteman's thunder was not pure, it did not give life.
The Old One had said,
"We must help the Gods.
We must send the Whiteman back where they came from.
They do not belong to the People,
They are not one of us."
The afternoon waited for the evening.
Bullets cracked and arrows flew.
Guns thundered and missiles whistled.
Bows twanged as projectiles hurtled toward the enemy,
the enemy of the Gods.
The hawk cried.
The deer bleated.
The beaver slapped his mighty tail.
Around the many fires the voice of the People spoke.
The tongues of flames carried the message
into the silence of the night, saying,
"It is our duty,
we are the People,
we must help the Gods."

FEAR

Time and circumstance unfold
and we present ourselves to each other.
A hierarchy of being emerges and persons are defined.
Seeking some soft, safe, sacred place to share our being,
we live with no sure way to tell
what any interchange will bring.
We continued to hunt for a place to live,
a place to share ourselves with others.
Centuries passed and we shared our thoughts and feelings,
still searching for some way to belong,
to be a part of something more than just us alone.
And yet we were always confronted
by languages we could not speak,
by clothes and customs that were strange,
by books we could not read.
Confused we roamed – pilgrimaged the globe,
never knowing who we or they really were.
The message from the Old Testament was
– fear the Other.
The message from the New Testament was
– love the Other.
A paradox still prevails as the messages conflict.
From chaos comes more chaos.
When will we become those free, open, sharing selves?
How are we to learn the secrets of this sharing?
We lie in beds and stare
at the randomness of the scattered forms.
The ragged shapes and round holes
are all we can distinguish on our acoustical ceilings.
There are no twigs or branches.

There are no planks.
There are no knots or grain to give us that knowledge,
some point of departure that says a season to all things.
We continue to stare and try to find some familiar shape,
some recognizable form.
If there were only knots –
knots are congealed life,
they burst forth as a branch,
shooting out and up, seeking something.
Words from some ancient tongue echo in my mind,
some long-ago message saying,
"I am the vine,
I am the trunk,
you are the branches."
Then we do belong! We do! We belong!
We are connected!
We come from someone!
We do not have to be afraid!
And yet …
To know where we came from is not enough.
We are tormented by the wonder of where we are going.
Mystics notwithstanding,
we are haunted by something ahead of us.
It must draw us towards itself.
It must draw us towards ourselves.
How can this happen?
Does this happen?
When am I one with the arrow and the bow?
When am I part of the infinite circle of being,
that eternal process that is not too large
for me to feel connected?

I listen for that orchestra
of which I must be a part.
I long for that feeling of being one with the music,
just one note now and forever.
A canto saying only,
"Amen!"

WAR

Under Heaven's Gate we war dogs wait.
Licking our wounds,
lapping at the ponds of time,
disturbing the still reflections of our deeds.
The oblivion of combat must have its birth in lost memories,
the scent of the hunt,
the thrill of the run,
the warmth of the kill.
And after the bison's dead,
an "I am!"
screamed into the unknown,
a momentary personal reprieve from death.
Comrades by the score lose life and limb.
Others scream,
cries deafen ears.
Villages and cities become heaped stone.
And still,
with burning zeal we shout,
"To Guernica and beyond!"
To what end, for what cause, do we spend
our very best?
Why by virtue of our presence,
do we think we're always right?
And in the end,
whose politic lights the Season's Fire,
holds the child's hand?

CONSUMED

The race is on.
Life is here.
Where to, my friend?
How long the journey?
Our feet beat upon the earth,
stumbling over the sacred and profane.
Beholding the beautiful and defiled,
we listen to peals of laughter and screams of pain.
An urgency of presence conflicts with self and circumstance.
Caught in the vortex of time and change,
we bleed.
Each beat of our heart
gives a measure of strength to soul and to purpose.
The pounding pushes us on and on.
We glance in haste and waste
as a rushing sense of self purges all serenity.
Seasons pass and leave us standing alone and still rushing,
our lives ebbing.
In flowing from the depths of self
we see so little as so much piles upon our heads,
the need to know and do
always screaming in our ears.
Breathing comes in shallow gasps.
Panting shakes our souls.
Still, drop by drop our lifeblood slips
through God's eternal hourglass.
The time has come when we are done.
Ravaged,
we moved in machinations.
Little did they do.
With life's blood gone, we die.

What magic softness is missing
from the blessed of the now?
Where have we been and where is it we must go?
Is the red of the fire lying just beneath the snow?
How long before the wind to cease,
the light to dim,
heart to stop,
the soul set free?
Lying in His Hallowed Hand,
Heaven's Gate is finally breached.
Eternal now,
we bathe in radiance – consumed in love.

ACADEMIA

Hallowed halls
Sinful corridors
Highest aspirations
Deepest depressions
The first
The last
The strong
The weak
The ideal
The mundane
Academics
Athletics
Serene reflection
Complete abandon
Galleries and books
Halls and crooks
Prudence
Prejudice
Virtue
Vice
Laughter
Pain
Green pockets
Paved lots
The patient
The rushed
Life
Interlude.

SANDUNGA

Brave hearts gracefully harboring courage,
an elegant presence in war.
Suffused in femininity a mortal commitment:
To be always at the sides of husbands and lovers.
Shawled shadows standing silently watching,
then gently stroking exhausted warriors.
Life as thin forms racked with weeping,
souls seeking some deep sentient confirmation.
Through screams of pain and the thunder of guns,
lying amidst drifting smoke and burning embers,
sharing warmth, food, and yourselves,
you live your lonely hours
close to the smell of earth and blood.
I see you kneeling in the waning twilight,
backdropped by candles flickering in the vespering dust.
The sounds of battle and pounding hearts
join the muffled whispers of your prayerful hope.
Stay! For God's sake!
You must remain in your chosen labor of love,
not for the madness of their efforts,
but for the essence of their dreams.

THE HEARTH

In the now we see, feel, and hear
MTV, T-Shirts, and Boom Boxes,
Connery,
Arnie,
and Sylvester,
Bruce,
Bruce,
and Banderas,
endless onslaughts.
In the then we saw, felt and heard
noise and fire,
a cadence,
shuffling feet of tired soldiers,
war forever abrupt and swift.
Silences shattered with yells and screams,
thunderous poundings of hordes and hooves,
thuds and blows, twangs of strings, whistling projectiles,
the agony of searing pain.
When will we see, feel and hear
the gentle licking of tongues, curling,
wrapped tightly to their fuel,
caressing, as it were, loving friends.
The sounds of combustion, constant and capricious,
a soft rushing of dancing flames, intermittent snaps,
hisses, the settling of embers,
and finally,
that last cascade of charcoal into ashes?

We need to see, feel, and hear the rhythm of the hearth,
to witness flutes and crenellations,
crevasses and caverns,
pockets of hidden, stored delight cast in a radiant glow,
a cloven end of log,
boars' snouts with tusks of flame,
gray-black lips of a dragon's grimace, sporting fire.
An awe-inspiring, reflective pause
giving us time to answer wonders
when souls are at risk.

FROM THE MOUTH OF THE CAVE

From the mouth of the cave
we stand gawking at the end of the day, into the setting sun.
Our face set agape in ignorance and awe.
The hours were spent burning, burning
in the mountains of Chiapas, on the planes of the Serengeti,
through the jungle of the Amazon.
Flames consume a piece of every continent,
save that mysterious frozen expanse
beyond the southern horizon.
And so, we also dumped untold tons of gallons
of poisons in the rivulets,
streams, rivers, lakes and oceans.
Then too, we belched toxins
into the air
of myriad pristine valleys.
Frenetic in our death pace, we rush back and forth,
up and down,
across and through, over and under our streets,
avenues, forests and planes,
shale and mountains, the seas and the stars.
Who would die if we all stood still?
Dumbfounded,
we watch life drip into the deserts of time.

VINCENT

They say your mood swings were too deep.
They say you were not whole.
To them I say,
"I would have held you in your moments of despair."
"He was ..."
Their prognostications fall like babble from shallow brooks.
I add,
"And I would have stood in awe
during your moments of ecstasy."
"The disease ..."
A litany of ignorance reveals paltry souls.
I would have given you my all in moments of need,
and complete freedom in your creative flights.
I hear they still say, "Depression and ... and ..."
You and I know that love's heights and depths
measure something else.
Thank you for your presence and your moments of pain,
and know that I am with you still, dancing in the rain.

THE FORMULA

Laboring with the essentials of life,
research:
A purpose – the controlling of disease.
Accidents occur.
Heard and seen, picked up by someone.
Sent out on the WWW – Thought to be close enough.
Whose? Mine? The investigator's?
Immediate acceptances on the WWW just because it's there.
Accolades, convocations, realizations
– then –
can so many be so wrong?
Who deceived whom?
The desire to know can have a pure heart and a blind eye.
The Real Truth always belongs to itself.
Finally, the Truth appears on the WWW.
Some will always believe what they see first
because that is what they choose to believe.
Others will blame deceit and become apathetic,
or worse still,
cynical.
A few will accept the shining Truth of the Now.
Moral:
Who's the victor?
Who's the race?
Who's the Truth Now?

OH – DANTE ALIGHIERI

In the twilight of the century
our remnants show their colors.
The movement of our kind stays the same:
Pilgrims and settlers, settlers and pilgrims,
faiths and deeds, lives and deaths,
shared events.
From the beginning of our time
life has been one with the other.
Cain and Abel, tribes and peoples,
north against south, east fighting west,
reason seeking faith, fundamentalism raging at change.
From the bones of eons, yesterday's newsprint,
and the media of the day,
atrocities scream across the millennia.
Those who participate in fratricide
forfeit their humanity in having no spirituality.
Edicts from the caverns of mephisto
rail against the holy endeavor of our presence.
Must we take again your journey
to behold a glimpse of virtue?

I

It's a blessed time when "I" becomes "we"
and everything's in IT.
Sidhartha knew it well
in the stench of the rotting crab.
I am the wind.
I am the hawk.
I am the rock.
I am the star.
Forever?
Yes/No/I do not know.
Am I a triad,
a duality?
I come from some place.
For how long?
Pushing, pushing, reaching, reaching, touching, touching
everything.
The rough, the smooth, the soft, the hard,
It and I becoming one.
Were we one before?
We must have been.
Being comes in me, through me, by me, and beyond me.
Will I continue to touch myself?
Does it matter?
There is no end; there is no beginning.
In, out, around and through, weaving forever,
the fabric of being clothes the universe.

TEARS

Cry! My people, cry!
Trails give birth to highways; canyons to lakes.
Listen to the echoes.
Look into the shadows.
Does the sobbing of the soul
match the timbre of the drum?

MONK'S MUTTERINGS

"I will place her chair next to his.
Who were they?
Who will they be?
All sisters,
all brothers,
I and the Father are one.
I will mark them,
so that
they will know."

* * *

From pure intent
– a gift of life to everyone –
the marks were made.
For years they sat empty
as lives were spent fearing desecration
of the Holy One.
Then, from abandonment,
they were rescued when one asked,
"Who to love?"
"Them all!"
thundered through the musty chapel.

THE HOMINID'S PATH

Potsherds, bits of flint, a bowl, an arrow head,
all labors' leavings
of the few and of the many.
Did we do enough?
How much was done?
And finally,
did we do too much?

WHO IS MY BROTHER AND MY SISTER?*

There is no such thing as new history –
there is only more history.
The savage, wanton maliciousness of the underbelly
of the snakes of humanity slither across the paths
of every generation, leaving trails in the dust.
May jackals tear at their gauntlets and their boots!
They came in the gentle light of the afternoon
and stayed into the soft dark of the night.
With blackened faces and camouflaged uniforms,
carrying weapons and full of the diabolical,
they came.
Cutting off the hands of God,
they slaughtered my father, my mother,
my brothers and my sisters,
all the men and women of my village.
They took away my history, my home.
I can no longer stand in the center of my surroundings,
feeling the presence of my own.
Everything has been taken from me.
I have become a disconnected vagabond,
death's gift to the living.
Only a soul remnant haunts me into lamentations.
How can I be touched by God
when they have cut off His hands?
Where is my family,
my friends, my neighbors?
The sacred trees were left splattered with
the blood of the unborn.

*Dedicated to all those who have lost their own in the onslaught of time and circumstances of history.

How can I stay on this ground
when the roots have been torn from my heart?
Only corpses and ashes lie where my village once stood.
I want in turn to slaughter them,
for them to become carrion, excrement of buzzards,
lying dead and dry upon the earth.
Yet how can I slay the demonic dragons of my kind,
when I know they are connected to someone –
when they were suckled at breasts and bathed in rivers?
New hope was born with them
and now they came into my sanctuary,
my life castle and …
Who told them to come?
Why did they listen?
How can a person betray their own kind?
They must learn to love before more of the innocent
are sacrificed on the altar of life.
Brush the brilliance in their hair, stroke their faces.
Touch them! Hold them!

* * *

I return in the spring to find my life's tattered relics.
They are not to be collected –
their cold presence could not touch me back.
Can I ever be touched when they have cut off His hands?
The Holy Truth is I am here now –
being touched by wounds and pain.
I cannot lay this suffering on another –
I will reach out and touch my brothers and my sisters.
I must become the hands of God.

YES?

And where are you?
I'm here! I'm there! I'm everywhere!
I'm laughing and I'm crying with Cervantes
and his knight's errant efforts
to lay to rest imagination and idyllic ethics,
while watching the current speculation on salvation.
I am with the Tutsis and the Irish,
with the Indios and the Bosnians,
the Eskimos and the many others.
I am with the persecuted and the starving,
the maligned and the depressed.
I am crying in the rain of time.
I am bashed upon the shore of a dry lake,
there are no waves of sentiment.
Where is the blanket of love to cover them all
and to dry their tears?

CONSPIRACY

Ideals and greed of the species
penetrate recesses of all creeds and colors.
The nobility of every beautiful kind
falls victim to methods of deceit.
Vain attempts to
"Bury it all"
in some peripheral and fleeting act of violence
erupt in the mundane passing of our days.
The Whole is touched by the few,
the few touched by the ONE
must scream,
"No! Not here! Not any longer!"
Although we hope for eternal quiescence,
we must shoulder an eternal vigilance.
From any place, any time,
a raging soul can lay claim to the innocent.
Destroyers of peace, counterfeiters of humanity,
always come.
Whirlwinds of chaos suck everything into their vortex,
leaving wounded hearts in their wake.
Why do we feel so inclined
to give passion its reign when we know
there is an after?

COLD LIGHT

Myriad lights from skyscrapers
cast shadows
among curving streets.
Bright eyes move on four wheels
as deep-throated monsters
weave idle patterns of complexity.
Rows of black squares
set in white facades
hang high up away from people.
I see all those little windows
and know
not one is mine.
All those cars
move by
with no one I know.
To stand alone in a huge city is like being naked in the dark
– vulnerable –
between you and it and them.

THE MALL

Throngs descend, search and buy, some just look.
Shapes, sizes and colors,
sharp contrasts, phasing shades,
all blending into one ocean of humanity.
Grandparents, babes in arms, sisters and brothers,
toddlers and tykes ("real" people, 6–8)
and hordes of teens all come.
In the early morning they come dribbling,
then form ripples in the midmorning,
becoming waves at noon,
followed by a tsunami in the early evening,
returning to waves and ripples, then dribbles,
and finally nothing.
From low tide to high to low they flow
while sweepers, like crabs,
swish debris into little flipper pails.
Some sashay, others saunter.
Many stroll.
A few pregnant, waddle magnificently.
Careening, pausing, studying, gently nudging, dragging,
pushing strollers filled with "almost people" trapped by straps.
Their eyes moving from movement to light,
stretching stubby fingers waving at sun catchers.
They pour through the Food Court –
for a culture that plays at eating –
only steps away from the 16 cinemas
able to transport anyone to the serenity of Montana.
From mundane to sublime,
we live bathing senses in waves of the human presence.

THE LAST MAN

I came upon a huddled, squatting form
beneath an old oak,
his back
next to the trunk.
He was alone.
The bent, frail, rugged form sheltered a bearded
and scared countenance
saturated with the lines of life.
Withered hands, the color of umber, were clasped in prayer.
Ragged, torn, and soiled clothes draped a wraith.
Who? What? Where? began the mind's incessant chatter.
Mutterings issued forth,
"Cyber Box, the Web, the Net …
No! No! Don't put me in!
We were just beginning to learn how to live,
had just started taking vacations
and enjoying shorter work weeks,
and realizing finally
we had to love all of the children."

FREEDOM

As I wander in the bustle of smog-shrouded freeways,
coming from the hinterlands of His garden,
I find I have lost my freedom.
I'm caught in a narrow causeway
following serpentine movement.
To go left, I cannot.
To go right is to risk life and limb
in the onslaught of the Others.
Stuck in an incessant flow
and an omnipresent roaring of radials,
I forget where I'm going.
I want only to stop, to rest,
to regenerate some semblance of life's spark.
Hollow cells have been driven empty
by ceaseless noise and movement.
My right becomes my left as the lane in which I'm caught
merges with five others.
The immediate task is to shelter myself once again
by crossing the lanes of the swift canisters of death.
Shocked from my monotonous survival mode,
I see flashing lights across the barricade,
stopped by a crushed vehicle.
Shattered back into a remnant of my senses,
blurry eyes refocus on my now tunneled escape route.
On a fleeting placard of a speeding new form of wagon
I see blazoned, "Torah."
Issuing from a deep forgotten soul crevasse
a feeble voice breaks forth,
"Adonai! Adonai!"

MEMORIES

Stark spire
standing undressed,
whose responsibility was left
undone?
To have been graced by Unfurled Glory was its only purpose –
and here, on an ordinary Tuesday at noon,
nothing hung from the naked post
save that simple cord used to carry aloft
the story of new beginnings
and boundless hopes.
Does history have its value,
or are we now wanderers on a new shore,
where raging waves of disconnected apathy
beat against a passionless desert?
Does it lie in a closet, or on a shelf?
Is simple space bedecked with forgotten treasure,
dust covered and folded into its triune form,
or just crumpled in a wrinkled heap?
Poignant Purpose, abandoned on this early spring day,
waits for someone to come and stand embarrassed
by the empty moment, remembering:
One must not beg for simple deeds
left forgotten among dying daffodils.

SEA SHELL

To what number of seasons
do we owe the strength of your swirls,
the soft hues of umber and cream,
your flutes, crenellations and escarpment?
The ridges of your undulations speak of ripples
and gentle fluctuations of tides.
Through how many days and nights,
lunar waxings and wanings,
temperature variations,
have soft secretions
congealed to make your home?
What consumed your flesh?
For whom were you sacrificed:
To the heart of God,
or the marauding carrion sweepers of the sea?
Are they the same?

* * *

To come to this –
fodder for child laborers
dusting their lungs as amulets
of night lights are created for nurseries.

* * *

In the orphanage
to each was given a carved shell
with the admonition:
Remember your sisters and brothers
laboring in sweat shops of screaming saws
and clouds of dust.

PIXEL STASIS

As we isolate ourselves into ourselves,
life's stream drains the heartland,
taking us from the loving touch
of parents, lovers, children, and friends –
those who buffered the omnipresent
push and pull of Eros and Thanatos.
From ecstasy's throes of union
to the desperate dread of loneliness,
we wander the pathways of our days.
Awe-struck and dumbfounded, we are caught
standing at sunsets in soft light,
then flattened by technology's capricious maelstroms.
Accompanied at times by gentle breezes
and fraught at others with gales,
we seek in wide-eyed innocence
and bleary-eyed apprehension
a bridge to forever "yes!"
In the cold expanse of life's new-found surf,
brothers and sisters search the Web for a warm embrace,
an escape from pixel stasis,
a techno bequeathed clicking Saint Vitus Dance,
a postmodern virulent virus causing
disorientation, fatigue, apathy,
and an agonizing emotional and spiritual death.
We were once called the proud crowd.
How could I be one of them
if I no longer know what I am,
or who you are?

* * *

Lost in the semi-dark fluoresced chamber
of my visual and audio mediated cubicle,
I sense only a fleeting memory of touch,
stimulated by ever-so-brief silent pauses
between the onslaughts of local and global bombastic noise
and racing eclectic movement.
Where is that quiet chapel hill
with vistas saturated with quiescence,
where from horizon to horizon
life stood bathed in hope and exercised in freedom?
Or is there now only a vague hybridized deity,
evolved from piles of information
and incessant vibrating electrons,
waiting to consume us in some form of gruesome sacrifice?

60s 70s 80s 90s ...

The jury has been coming in for some time:
We, the different members of the human species, are not well.
The prescription drugs topping the current global list are
Prilosec and Prozac.
The fraternal twins of anxiety and depression
seek to destroy great numbers of us.
As we share our timebeing, the rational social animal's,
the homofaber's, the symbolizing one,
the sentient soul, the freedom seeker with others,
many become collateral damage of the implosion.
The pace of the day,
bounded by omnipresent noise and movement,
disorients us in its onslaught.
We disintegrate in a new form of devolution.
"Get your life (act) together!"
"Don't lose it!"
"You're losing it!"
"You've lost it!"
And if it's all a play,
we buy into a presentation
that comes before us
and behind us,
leaving us standing
exhausted in a twilight of never-never.
Who will say gently, firmly, and finally, "No!"
And who will stop long enough to feel or hear the question?
Not much learning takes place in strobed dim light,
amidst excessive libations,
and the raging infernal noise of a discotheque.

VOICES OF HUMANKIND

How many screams have the stones
(in the cells of time)
absorbed?
All of them?
None of them?
Tell us!
Still we hear and feel echoes' reverberations
through centuries' halls,
rattling sensitivities and forcing blood from our bones.

* * *

Founding blocks of social change must work their way
through the Trivium of human fortresses:
[Think] [Say] [Do].
Millennia must pass
before a foundation deep enough
has been constructed
upon which the first wall
of a truly global temple
may be built.

MOTHER NATURE

O holy truths,
where are your believers?
Echoes of silence come as crescendos.
Where have they all gone,
those hominids that populated the land?
I feel reverberations of stillness.
O Holy One, will this be the Great Awakening?
Is this the moment of transition
when the land speaks and we finally hear –
wailings of whales, howlings of wolves,
cries of songbirds?
Have we reached the precipice of the
mechanic/electronic archipelago?
Can we finally separate ourselves from the trail of machines?
Will the insufferable movement
of whirring vibrations and the scent of hot air,
– double gifts of heated motors and cooling fans
surrounding electrons –
ever stop and be silent?

THE RIGHT

From whence the age's wisdom
that spills upon the human path?
Men to men,
man to man,
man to boy,
comes evolution's seminal efforts.
To know who you are is everything.
To learn the right kind of courage for every place,
time and circumstance
is the only purpose.
When and where to fight,
about what to commit a soul's energy
is paramount.
And so ...
The night rider swooned at the moon.
The dawn rider embraced the day.
The noon rider basked in the sun.
The dusk rider sat awe-struck before the stars.
From time's cave drift the strains of an eternal flute
echoing through the fabric of the silent cosmos
whispering,
"Biophilia! Biophilia!"

LIFE'S JOURNEY

Age-dependent information
waits and waits for the right moment
– then –
when it arrives a light shines upon
THE TRUTH
and we turn away from past perceptions,
seeing for the first time what is eternally already there.
Meanwhile, children – ever so egocentric –
watch and wait as inexorable human tides
ebb and flow, covering, bearing, taking, giving.
What values are we to hold
when "others" are so different?
We have watched the many acts of the human drama
and have oft concluded:
Right thing, wrong time and all of the reciprocals
that logic and that thin film of experience
have sought to bestow on the always limited perspectives
of the species' mind and heart.
Culture's trappings,
caught in blood-stained and wind-whipped cloaks
always providing too little understanding and warmth,
have seduced us into beliefs
often shallow, less than magnanimous,
darkening our visions of self and others.
Intra and inter group struggles,
as with all racial clashes,
have always looked at each other
through short-sighted vision
weaned on ignorance and colored with lust or fear.
Cain against Abel,
brown against brown,
white against white,
black against black,
then everyone against each other and against the yellow.

Know this!
The Sleeping Giant has always cast her children into the sea.
Forever landing upon new shores
they came to learn new things,
and taught old things,
things they never forgot.
Always the same in every language, every culture:
Life's passion for itself lingers at the edge of life's vision.
The responsibility of our current moment
predicates a communal interface
that must limit the participation
of the deranged and fanatical.
Biophilia must be the common denominator
as we close the circle
of our species' diaspora.
Our dedication must be:
Recapture the vision!

DISTURBING THE PEACE

Where, oh where is peace?
Communities of the new century meet in Mega Malls
– before and after –
the movies.
Is there some erosion, degradation of human life,
when piercing noise envelops everyone in every space?
We sit in jets for hours listening to headphones
and the roaring onslaught of engines.
Who speaks of jet lag,
disorientation, assaulted senses?
Vibrations shatter the diligent rhythms
of organisms' gentle play.
How much more of evolution's gifts
of pace, peace, and silence
must we lose?

TO THOSE WHO LOST …

It need not be said,
but must be remembered:
Hearken to all those who fought in lost wars
– lest we forget –
the victors may be far less
than the vanquished ever were.

REFUGEES

How far from the heart of the whole must they be
before we recognize the difference?
Our egocentric selves,
lost in our ethnocentric histories,
see so little in the differences we purport to *Others*.
How far they are from us,
we say in those seldom moments of reflection.
When does the "I" stop its self-circumnavigation and peer out?
When does our fear of losing "one" let go long enough
for us to see something different?
In those holy times when immersed in "It"
we cry out for oneness
and It presents itself in the Other.
Finally, our beleaguered soul snaps to a cold attention
and we see, feel, and hear the cries
of our brothers and our sisters.
Their moaning almost upsets us – until,
in that sacred crucible of truth,
the mighty smithy hammers out a reflection of ourselves.
From the depths of cultural archetypes
we emerge to stand naked in a whirlpool
of consciousness' stream,
and in that nakedness we come face to face
with the agony and ecstasy of belonging all to "It."
From munificence to beneficence
the tick-tock of our awareness becomes a silence
melting into everything.
Then a cacophony of yeses screamed into our ears
rages through us, leaving in their wake
a still point of reflection
in which we behold the face of God.

SOUL'S SEARCH

If, when we sit and watch old men
we can know that some of them are contemplating
the importance of knowing the difference
between "here" and "there,"
we are way ahead in the game.
Everything always lies between here and there
in space and time, in heart and mind.
We can know we've been there, or want to go there,
or be there.
And yet we are forever here.
Dreams are to teach humility and patience and courage,
above all, courage in the face of unbelievers
and the weaknesses of the Hidden One.
So ...
Please let them all know there is always a place in time
when we don't want to go there.

I WANT …

To be an antihistorian.
To fight the face of immutable time.
To withstand the winds of history whose gales perturb
our nows and whose clouds keep the *right* from view
to create a life that thresholds on today and embraces
the hallowed simplicity of
THE TRUTH NOW!

A HUMAN FACE – A HUMAN TOUCH

As we step into the next millennium,
awash in the wake of the post-industrial,
postmodern,
electronic media-saturated environment,
we must be ever vigilant.
Evolution has taken such a wonderfully long time
to get us here –
through interstellar trails of primeval dust and muck.
Now,
thresholding into the future
as co-participants in the creative process,
we are faced with,
as always,
the opportunity to maintain an ever-present commitment
to what personhood is all about.
A fleeting, incessant blip on our intellectual, emotional,
physical and spiritual horizons
hints of an unknown presence shadowing us.
Something always has –
The gods? Evil spirits?
Now that God is dead and evil spirits
the entertainment of children and teenagers,
what is it that blows the winds of turbulence,
shakes our tree,
shadows our sunny days?
What eclectic movements do we fear?
What dissonance absorbs our senses?

The venues of the day's exposure
come from an implosion of people
(other beings present in our known space)
and data coming from everywhere
and overloading all of our senses.
Numbers,
beyond the simple,
are incomprehensible (except to a few)
and therefore, without our comprehension, meaningless.
Yet ...
the presence of others,
different others,
(only in that naive historical sense)
is disconcerting.
We don't feel connected.
Something tells us we should,
we are all brothers and sisters,
and yet ...
we really aren't quite sure how we
go about that magnanimous interface.
In any case,
we have too much on our plates.
And the banter,
informative and noxious of all kinds,
soothes, assaults
and otherwise floods our commuting time
while punctuations of music(?)
occupies our ears and boom boxes carried on four wheels
invade our space, causing disturbing sensations.
Is any of this understandable,
or are we all by default
"buying"
the postmodern dissonance as the only truth?
If it sells it must be good.

The truth has become a market-driven commodity,
hasn't it?
Projectiles of jacketed lead death abound,
methods of delivery are available through mail order
to almost everyone.
Tons of ordnance,
(the equivalent of so much TNT)
including those insidious antipersonnel land mines,
still lie scattered about
as we wander aimlessly into tomorrow
surrounded by the omnipresent
Data Smog* of the day.
To whom can we turn for answers?
Where can we look for that special interface,
that process called higher formal
(does formal have meaning anymore?) education,
and see a human face and feel a human touch?
It must be more or less than virtual reality
(now that's an oxymoron).
Something is either real as a creation, or an invention,
that although "real"
isn't
really real.
Ah, but who can tell,
some say it is
and maybe they are right.
And I don't want to be embarrassed with my ignorance.
God knows
(that's only a figure of speech, now, of course)
I don't know everything.
But I do, at some level, know what I think I like.

*Data Smog, David Shenk.

So …
when I think about it
(that pastime of reflecting with an honest wonder),
"It,"
sharing being in time (real now-time for most of us) must,
if we reflect long enough about our *real* comfort zone
(with self and others),
be doable, rewarding and regenerating.
It all must be more than a media transformed into a medium
becoming a message.
It must be a transubstantial exercise of shared being
melting into one
and that one,
for most of us,
must have predominantly real time,
real life attributes.
Our universities for the next millennium must be personal.
They cannot be too cold,
they must be warm enough.
They cannot be too hard,
they must be soft enough.
We are that rational social animal, the homofaber,
the desirer of freedom,
a symbolizing, soul-seeking sentient being
who in the courses of our species' journey
must forever size personhood to itself.
We must be very close (close enough) to who we *really* are,
not simulacra ad nauseam.
After all,
how many of me can there *really* be?
Just one!

We know the "times they are a'changin'."
So they have been saying and so they are
and yet, with each ripple on the pond
of the serenity of our aspirations,
we feel more than a little disturbed.
Echoes in the winds of time
repeat the age-old rational/social dictum:
How much is too much and how much is too little?
To this we must pay attention.
We (some of us) have bought
at the physical level
the "use it or lose it" mandate.
Now we MUST extend this commitment
to the other three theaters of our personhoods:
The intellectual, emotional and spiritual.
So we may ask ...
How many tools do we need and of what kind?
At what pace must we labor and for what purpose?
To whom and what do we dedicate our very best
as we attempt to share the knowledge of the ages
so that we may enhance our Now?
Are we able to protect ourselves and our children
from donning victimhoods of our blind machinations
as the Internet's tentacles gather in force and kind?
The answer MUST be a forever yes!
Yes! And yes again!
To ignore the hard-won wisdom of history is more than foolish,
it is life threatening and not just to us here now,
but to all those children,
"the forever young that come and come and come,
wide eyed and innocent,"
truly victims.

We MUST choose not to sacrifice them on some altar of the marketplace.
We must touch them and look into their faces and say, "Yes! Yes! And yes again!"
Yes! To the beauty of each one!
Yes! To the doability of our *real selves*!
Yes! To the current crown of humanity
with its multicolored, multilingual, multicultural, multifaceted personhood!

ADORATION

I am a microcosm – the macrocosm comes into being
through me.
It exists without me and yet I witness its caring movement.
That is to say – things have their own time and space
and so do I.
My purpose is to be me, a man from a mother and a father,
grateful for the opportunity to witness
from my small cell window
the flowing of the Father's robes.
That He cares, I see, because remnants of all things move
toward themselves and toward Something Else.
A torrent is laid upon the valley.
The clashing of the heaven's bowels has ceased.
Before me across the garden stands a pine
and behold – silver droplets cling to the tip of each needle,
mirrors for the afternoon's dying movement.
The menagerie of spheres captures points of golden light,
from One to many to one and back to One.
I share Your presence.
Society – many of me –
beyond the limits of yesterday's brief local focus,
lungs and blood,
temples pound, caught in the paradigm of today.
Anxiousness permeates every movement and reflection.
A scream among the herd,
"NO! NOT THIS!"
It's theirs, not mine! They must choose! I have chosen!
"YES! THIS, NOW!"
It's mine! For me! I must own it!
They are wandering.
I must tell them to stop
and listen to the voices of the shoulders of the day.

MOURNING SONG

The Truth of the Greater Good
must extend through us and beyond us to the All.
We must wait upon the Truth before we condemn
our brothers and our sisters.
Remember, patience gives us prudence
and the ability to see and do.
A cancerous few affect the many
as the mitochondria of the miraculous nets and penetrates
the fabric of the species.
Know this:
We must learn to excise the cancers!
Why this appalling outbreak of senseless abandonment
by members of our own kind?
We wonder how much of this we owe to God and yet,
we have to turn to ourselves and ask,
"Did we touch them enough?"
Every mother, father, brother, sister has that mandate:
"Love is touch."

* * *

Helping hands coalesced from divergent cities.
Grief poured in from around the world.
Why innocent victims?
Where is the logic of the Divine Plan?
A sandal, a tennis shoe
will never again know their warm, soft owner's foot.
Mothers' and fathers' arms hang empty.
Parents, friends, relatives and associates
have lost their loved ones.

By the thousands they gathered,
sharing gentle touches and soft words.
Some with set jaws, some with moist eyes,
all sitting in many rows,
making a statement with their presence.
The nation's muted note was played on electronic airways.
The multitudes listened to inspirational overtures,
songs of mourning,
all seeking understanding for a hungry hope.
Messages crackled in from other places:
"Who will cry for the Hutu and the Tutsi?"
Simple reminders came to tell us,
the victims are many and diverse.
Can we *finally* own the Truth of One in the Now?
The few were recognized by many.
When will the many be eulogized by us all?
Do trembling children, wide eyed and frightened,
finally touch deep enough our hearts, our minds,
our bodies and our souls?
The world is a potpourri of the species,
melting into one, becoming a flowing river,
forever bringing brothers and sisters to new shores.
Hear this:
When anyone is lost there must be a ripple
on the waters of our kind.
We must know the tender touch of children,
must never forget the tender touch of children.
They are for whom we toil,
they are the recipients of our good and evil acts.
God!
"Please bless the children!"

STRIKE FORCE

More than just enough,
less than too much,
life threads the needle of the possible.
From a democracy of biology and our own kind
rings a message:
"All *men* are created equal"
and *still* "we are engaged in a Great Civil War
testing whether *that nation*, or *any nation* so conceived
and so dedicated
can long endure."
On the altars of our battlefields the value of the species
becomes a holy sacrifice.
The rational animal's personal integrity encompasses
a universal commitment to life:
A life which begets and fosters more life,
and yet, not all life.
The cancers of our now and future,
many the gifts of progress and numbers,
are set to assail the soft tissue of fellow travelers.
We ride on a spaceship
that is not responsible for its privileged inhabitants.
Therefore we must develop a resolve:
Surgery is a must, cancers must be removed.
Healthy flesh will be invaded and infringed upon.
The living paradox: Yes/No.
Life's mandate: Some yes/All no,
Enough of everything/Not too much of anything.
The mystical demands participation
in the paradox of the existential totality.
The execution of our presence can only be done
with the law of love.

In seeking the Truth of the Now
we must get close enough
to the edge of God's mind
without losing sight of our souls.
Our challenge is to train soldiers for surgical strikes,
while attuning minds of citizens
to know when to send them into theaters of operation,
and to support them while they are there
and to welcome them home when they are done.
Existence is *educere*,
the leading out of complex Truths
from within and without,
all becoming in the present.
Unless we choose to maintain a commitment
to excise the insidious malevolence
of our brothers and our sisters,
we will not be able to exert control and deterrence
at the heart and periphery of our kind.
Freedom and restraint lie in the balance:
Close enough, swift enough,
Now!

THE WOUNDS OF HUMANITY

We sit in pools of soul blood.
Our moving hands shadowed in the moon's reflection
are cast in a cold silver.
We cannot remove the daggers from our hearts.
The harder we pull,
the faster they stay.
In the morning we thought we heard a voice
and believed we understood impassioned sharing.
In the afternoon
we felt the thrust of the blade
and a ravaging wind.
We thought we were soft chamois
used to polish gold.
Now,
we feel like dirty old rags
shaken and discarded.

SWORD AND SHIELD

He stood.
The clarion's call was clear.
He turned
with countenance set.
The weighty mail moved.
A heavy sword was drawn.
The visor dropped.
A polished shield gleamed.
The Knight's blue eyes pierced the dim light of the dawn.
In the distance forms moved.
Dark grotesque shadows slid from tree to tree
towards the edge of the glen.
He saw them, four in all.
The ledge upon which he sat guarded his back.
Finally, rays of rising sun touched the field.
Screams and moans came from the lifting mist.
The attack was at hand.

* * *

Patience and practice had given birth to a mighty will.
Prudence reigned in a fierce heart.
Faith in the Truth of One guided a sure sword
and a solid shield.
Life's path leading always to the wizards of sin.

* * *

Wandering hearts converged on the dew-laden, rutted road.
She came stooped with her heavy basket and shuffling feet.
He moved slowly, bent before the axle of his cart.
Cast-down eyes saw nothing of the present danger.

What meager defense was carried in the pockets of their souls?
In that last brief silence before the splitting of the day,
beating weary hearts locked wills to visions
beyond their current circumstance.
Life's brilliance suffered deep the burdens of the past.
Loves lost and torn from breasts too young
were too much to bear, too much for hope.
Death was overtaking life before its time,
despair their only cloak.

* * *

The monsters now came rushing from their hidden caves,
screeching vile obscenities against the One.
Encircling wounded prey they pounced.
The Knight's gentle resonating voice cracked through the din.
"Not today!" was all he said.
With sword in swing he assailed the throng.
From deep within his golden heart a fire lit the battlefield.
The whistle of his swift blade breathed a song of love.
Blinded by their victimhoods they stumbled,
clouds of fear, anger, guilt and false pride
shrouded weary eyes.
Depressed into life,
forms bore no semblance of recognition.
Slicing through vicious blows,
he stood between the wounded souls.
She cowered at his feet.
He slunk behind his mighty form.
To the young lady, "Never on thy knees to me!" he said.
Pulling the young man to his side he breathed,
"The Truth is Now!"
The slithering smoke-belching forms merged.
A fire-breathing dragon with four heads stood before them.

"And now," the Knight said, "Your death!"
The battle raged.
She grabbed his sword.
He latched onto his shield.
"Let go!" he said,
as the dragon's heads spit smoke and fire.
She screamed, "It burns my eyes, I cannot see!"
He bellowed, "The smoke, I cannot breathe!"
In a gentle voice the Knight said,
"You must let go of my sword and shield."
Shaking in fear they complied.
Swinging his mighty blade
the Knight cut off
one of the monster's heads.
"You will never be afraid again," he said.
"But there are others and they will kill us!"
they both shouted angrily.
"Silence!" was all they heard.
Stepping out, the Knight rammed forward his shield.
One of the monster's heads, bashed bloody,
dangled helplessly on the great body.
"We are sorry," they murmured.
"Of guilt you shall have none!"
was thundered down through screams.
"But we have sinned!" they moaned.
"I left my love for the chance to dance,"
she whispered.
"I left my lady for a road to travel,"
he gasped.
"Where are you now?"
asked the Knight.

"Here! Right here!"
they shouted.
The Knight's heavy sword severed another head.
"I wish I could go back," she said.
"Me too," he added.
"Is that true?" the Knight asked.
"Yes! Oh yes!"
was all they uttered.
With one final blow the last head was separated
from the monster.
The huge body swung flailing around the three.
"And now," the Knight queried,
"What will you do?"
"Find my love," she breathed.
"Yes, I will return to my heart's life," he murmured.
The Knight held his shield towards the light of the sun
and simply said, "See!"
In that instant both saw their lost loves reflected
in the burnished shield.
Rushing into each other's arms,
they fell to weeping and issued cries of joy.
Fatigued, the Knight stood breathless.
The monster's strength wore upon him.
With torn mail and ravaged arm he urged them
to pick up his shield and sword.
She finally took up the shield.
He bent down and picked up the sword.
The headless, faltering beast closed upon them.
She held steady the shield, bearing its heavy weight.

He made one deep thrust with the Knight's sword,
slicing though the underbelly,
piercing its heart.
The great body quivered and fell dead.
"Now," the old Knight said,
"You will never be afraid, angry, guilty,
or suffer any false pride.
The monsters are all dead.
Forget the past.
Look into the shield of love and tell me what you see."
"My love," they both sighed.
"Yes, that is all you see in the Now.
Remember this – the Truth of One in the Now
is all that matters.
Know thyself and to thine own self be true.
From this moment forward,
finally having found your souls,
take each other by becoming one with yourselves.
It will take time to practice the virtues,
schedule prayers when you are alone
and when you are together.
You have just learned the most important thing:
Love the Truth of One Now more than anything
And share this truth with your love."
The old Knight helped the young lady put her basket
in the young man's cart.
They both took hold of the handle and began to pull together.
Turning to thank the Knight,
all they saw was his broad back walking slowly
towards the cliffs of stone.

They had touched his Shield of Love
and held his Sword of Truth.
His heavy arms were now hanging gently at his sides.
He moved towards the cliff's wall
to stand again for mercy's sake,
a mighty form ready to do battle for
the Truth of One in the Now.

* * *

And so it was,
the old Knight waited in his dutiful role,
battling the wizards of sin,
and stayed in his chosen place, at his appointed task.
He looked forward to his sole social fare,
weekly visits from an old monk.
The Abbot's seminal sojourn took him by
the old Knight's station.
They shared the Mass under the beauty of the day,
or in weather, in a small grotto near the ledge.
The old Knight deeply relished the soul-serving, sacred meal
of bread and wine.
After their mutual sanctification they would sit and share,
conversation always turning to the beauty of God's ways,
the grace in their lives,
and gifts they were able to share with others.
Meals were the simple remains of the gifts of passersby.
The years drifted by.
Days of reflection brought the old Knight to wondering
how many of the helped souls went on with their lives,
giving assistance to others.

He speculated that if they could,
some day everyone would be about helping others.
The thought warmed his old body and sparked
an Alleluia
within his soul.
As the seasons came and went the aging Knight
and Monk saw fewer people in their remote
corner of the world.
More time was spent in prayer and fasting.
It came to pass ...
One day the old Monk called up to the cliff's edge
and there was no response.
Laboring up the well-worn path, the old Monk
came upon the truth:
Seated on his cliffside bench of stone,
the old Knight was dead.
His grim soft features were now akin to
the stone against his back.
He held his shield hanging slightly off his knee.
As the Abbot gazed into its polished surface,
he saw a golden, wavering light.
Reflected were two figures: a resplendent gentle man
and a young Knight.
Transfixed before the scene,
the Monk fell upon his knees, offering praises to
The Most Holy.
As twilight drifted in, rising from aching knees,
he began to gather stones.
Slowly he formed them and surrounded
the sitting Knight in his tomb.

* * *

In the years to come the story spread,
one could see – if they stood just right –
a brilliant, gleaming light,
an emanation from deep within the stone.
An enveloping feeling of freedom pervaded any soul
that stood before the shrine.
A lifting of fear, anger, guilt and false pride
would set souls singing in sheer joy.
Prayers were offered to unknown gods as weary travelers,
lost from life's busy highways,
stumbled down the long forgotten path.

* * *

An ancient couple came slowly through the glen,
followed by a young man and young woman.
Conversation passed from winded elders to youthful spirits.
"Here is where it was," they said.
The young ones had heard the story
from their grandparents many times over.
They gazed across the hillsides seeking any form.
Suddenly, there upon the hill was a brilliant flash.
Rushing up the steep slope, the young man and the young lady
came to an old tomb.
"Here!" they shouted to the old couple.
Struggling legs were lifted by gentle-hearted souls
as they clasped each other's hand.
Mounting the perilous incline, they knelt before the shrine.
"Hear now the Truth again," they said.
The story of their encounter with the old Knight
many years ago
captured anew the young ones' imaginations
as they sat in this sacred place.

Tears welled from old eyes and cascaded down
weathered and worn cheeks.
Hands were held as sacred troths were again
pledged to loving ears.
The youngsters, dropping to their knees, said,
"A Holy Thing did happen here."

* * *

A voice from deep within the stone said,
"Remember the Truth of One in the Now."
"We have remembered," the old couple whispered.
"We will remember," was confirmed in unison
by the young man and the young lady.
A streak of golden light split the evening's shadows
as gentle spirits walked upon the land.
A radiant, white form flanked by a young Monk
and a young Knight were singing,
"No fear, no anger, no guilt, no false pride –
never again for anyone!"
The celestial chorus went on with fading words.
The young couple strained their ears to hear.
"One … Silence … See … Truth … Now … Love …
Growth … Holy Endeavor …"
Lives would forever be changed,
would forever belong to
The Mystery of One in the Now.

www.ingramcontent.com/pod-product-compliance
Lightning Source LLC
Chambersburg PA
CBHW051805040426
42446CB00007B/531